Catjectives

Written by Arlene Maguire

Illustrated by Janie Stapleton

To my four outstanding grandchildren,
Mary, Oliver, Jack and William

Catjectives -

a word that defines or describes cats.

Aa

Agile (a-jil) - nimble, spry, deft, graceful

Agile Andy walks the gate.
Fish for dinner. Can't be late.

Bb

Blasé (bla-zay) - unexcited, indifferent, unmovable, laid back

Blasé Barry naps in the sun.
It's his idea of having fun.

Cc

Curious (cur-ee-us) - nosy, prying, snoopy, inquisitive

Curious Carly's head is stuck,
She wants out. Wish her luck!

Dd

Dapper (dap-per) - chic, dashing, classy, good-looking

*Dapper Dan thinks he's best...
Much, much better than the rest!*

Ee

Entertaining (en-ter-tay-ning) - amusing, funny, playful, clownish

Entertaining Eddy sure
makes us giggle.
Twisted in yarn,
with a funny wiggle.

Ff

Flexible (flek-si-bul) - stretchy, supple, limber, acrobatic

Flexible Freddie stretches out. Pushing and turning all about.

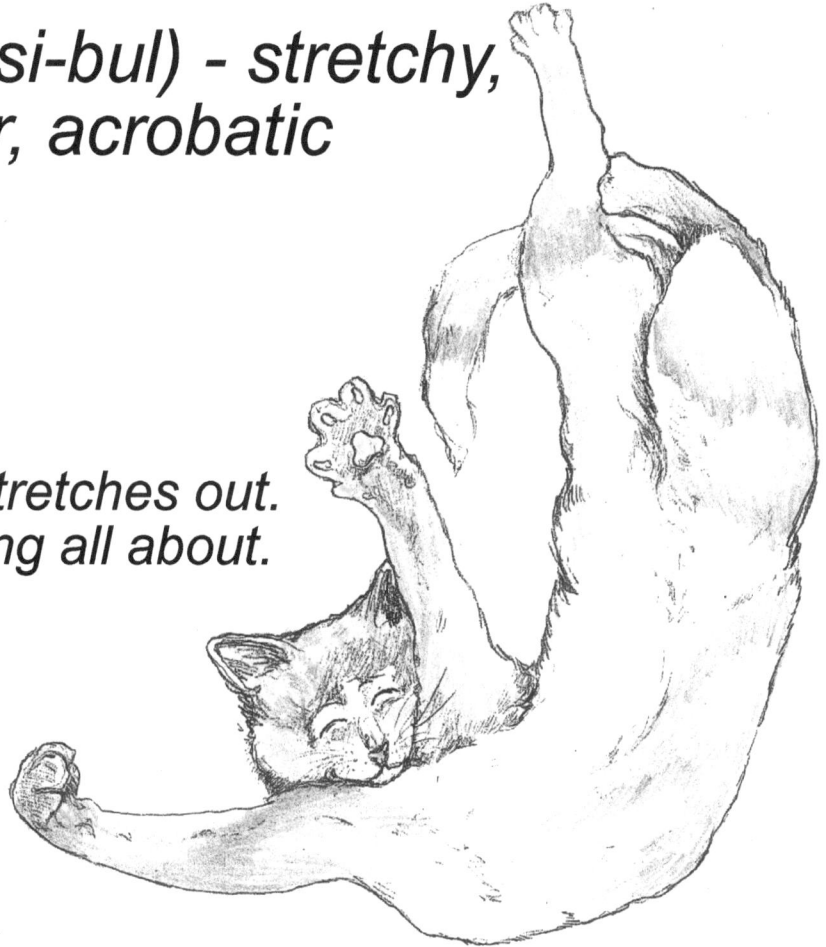

Gg

Grandiose (gran-dee-ose) -
great, fabulous,
splendid, magnificent

Grandiose Greg wants
you to know,
He won a ribbon
at the show.

Hh

Hygienic (hi-gen-ik) - clean, scrubbed, well-washed, healthful

Hygienic Helen cleans her paws, Careful to avoid her claws.

Ii

Indifferent (in-dif-er-ent) -
cool, unruffled, serene, not caring

Indifferent Irwin doesn't mind.
That barking dog is not so kind.

Jj

Joyful (joi-ful) - happy, merry,
delighted, cheerful

Joyful Jan attacks the mouse
Scooting and skidding around the house.

Kk

Keen (keen) -
clever, bright,
smart, sharp

Keen kitty Kenny
takes a peek,
Thinks you're playing
hide and seek.

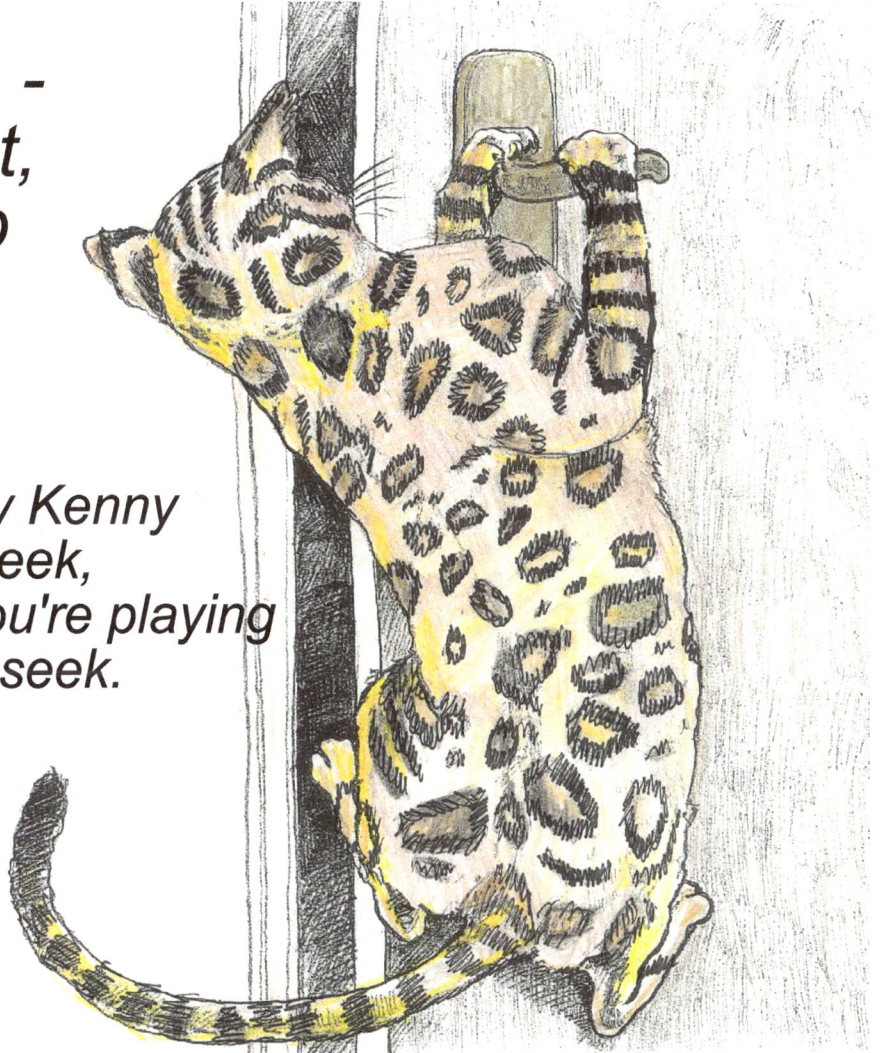

Ll

Lovable (luv-uh-bul) - adorable, cute, sweet, precious

Lovable Lily waiting to eat.
Such a good kitten deserves a treat.

Mm

Mischievous (mis-chi-vus) -
naughty, impish, playful, teasing

Mischievous Milo
teases the fish
Paw in the water.
Swish, swish, swish.

Nn

Nurturing (nur-chur-ing) - caring, guarding, protecting, nursing

Nurturing Nelly carries her kit.
Running for safety, lickety split.

Oo

Odd (ah-d) - rare, unusual, different, uncommon

Odd Oliver without hair.
A special cat that's very rare.

Pp

Patient (pay-shent) - easy-going, kind,
gentle, calm

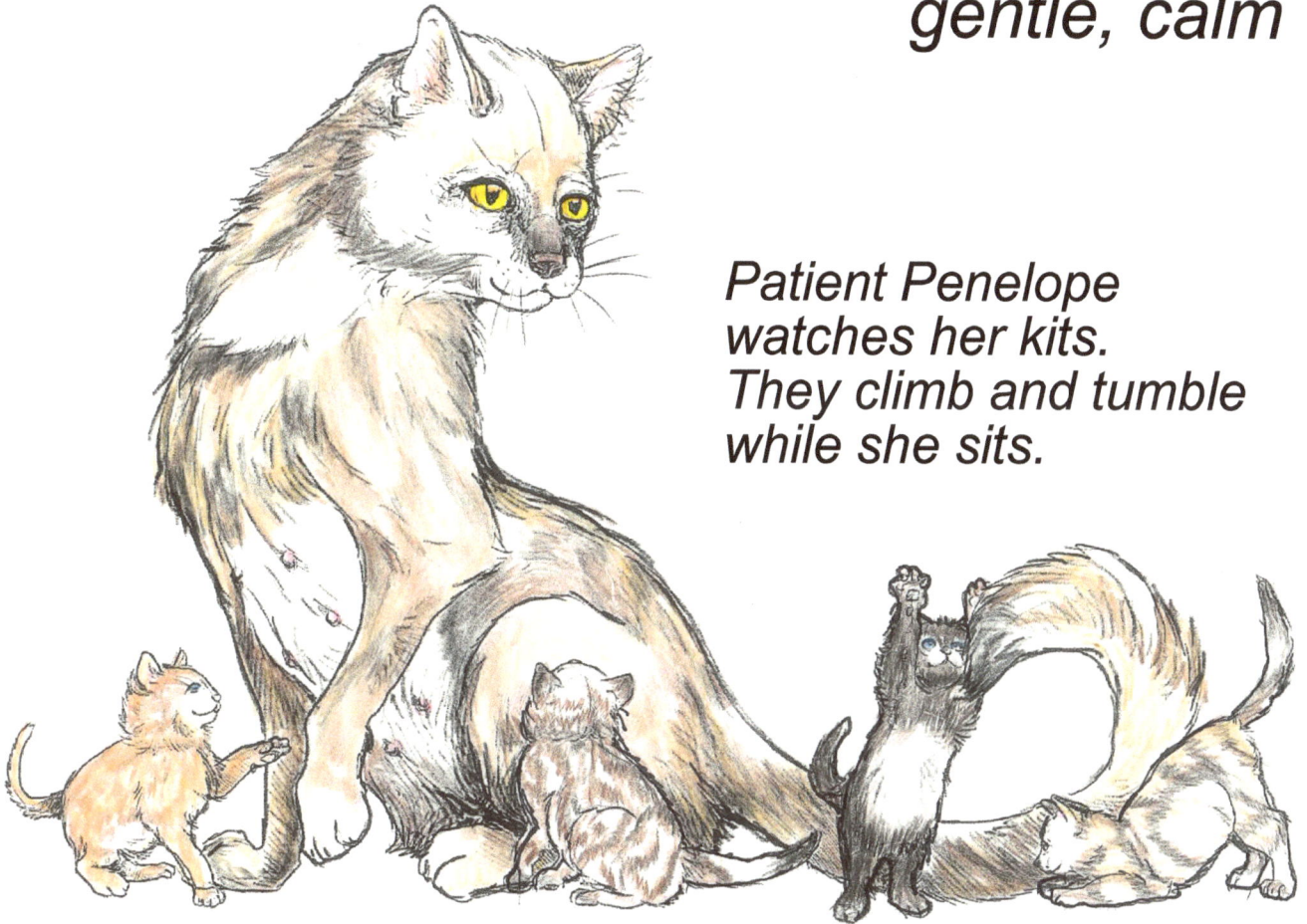

Patient Penelope
watches her kits.
They climb and tumble
while she sits.

Qq

Quarrelsome (kwor-el-sum) -
fighting, crabby, brawling, bickering

Quarrelsome Quentin picks a fight.
The frightened cat will soon take flight!

Rr

Roving (rov-ing) - roaming, strolling, rambling, prowling

Roving Romero wanders away.
Will he come back? Who can say?

Ss

Spasmodic (spaz-mah-dik) - fitful, restless, erratic, flighty

Spasmodic Spencer dashes past.
Going, going way too fast!

Tt

Tough (tuf) - mighty, rugged, sturdy, strong

*Tough Tommy
acting mean,
Angriest cat
you've ever seen!*

Uu

Unique (you-neek) - special, one-of-a-kind, matchless, unequaled

Unique Umberto - heart on his chest, That makes him different from the rest.

Vv

Valued (val-ud) - prized, treasured, cherished, appreciated

Valued Valerie
sits alone,
A queen upon
her velvet throne.

Ww

Wary (wehr-ree) -
careful, cautious, guarded, suspicious

Wary Warren's a
scaredy cat.
Oh my goodness!
What is that?

Xx

Xantic (zan-tik) - yellow, sandy-colored, honey-colored, golden

*Xantic Xena's
a tabby kitty.
With golden fur,
sweet and pretty.*

Yy

*Yowling (yow-ling) -
crying, yelling,
wailing, screaming*

*Yowling Yuri
crying and whining,
He'll quiet down
once he is dining.*

Zz

Zany (zay-nee) - daffy, laughable, comical, funny

Zany Zack -
Oh, what a sight,
Keeps us laughing
day and night!

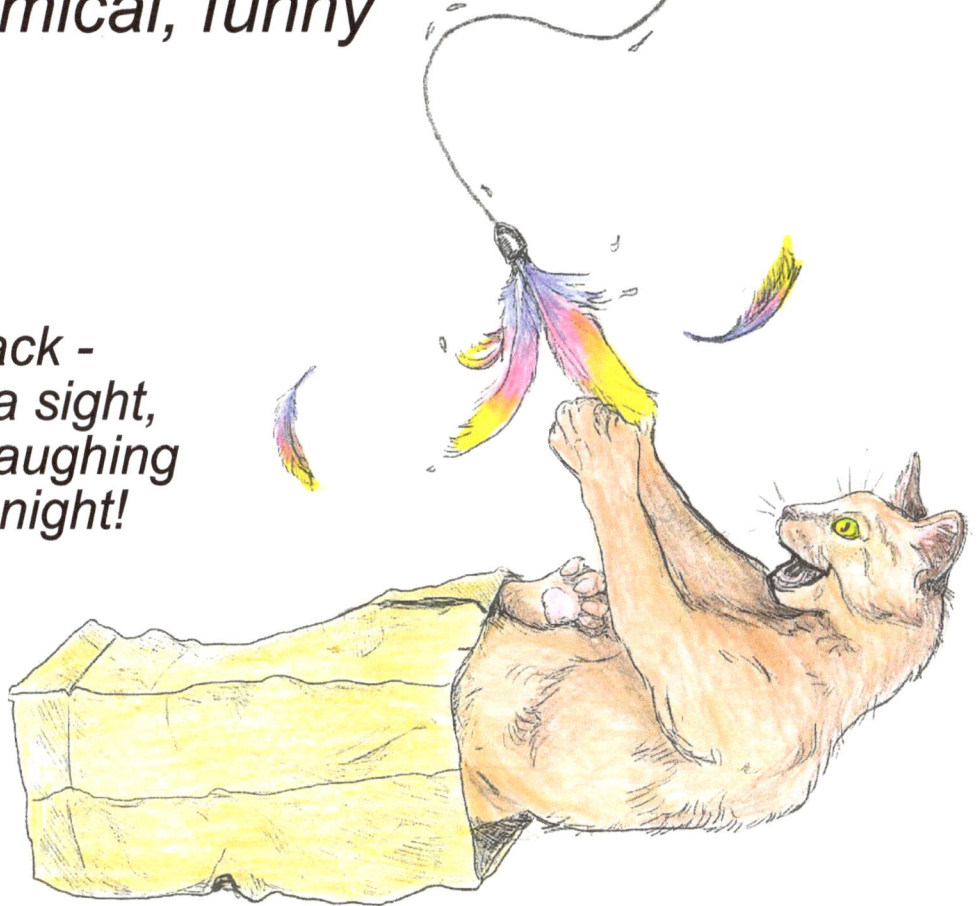

Acknowledgements

Thank you to the amazing souls who helped me edit Catjectives, Penelope Fox and Phee Sherline.

Arlene Maguire, born in Newark, New Jersey, is a cum laude graduate of Rutgers University, where she earned her teaching degree.

After working with elementary school students, she began writing picture books. Arlene has published seven books for children, with well over 100,000 sold internationally. In 2009, her book, *Special People, Special Ways*, won the Preferred Choice Award.

Many of her lyrical books help build self-esteem, while others are educational and just for fun. You can see many of Arlene's books on Amazon and Barnes and Noble.

Having moved to California and ready for a career change, Arlene started an insurance agency with her youngest daughter. Her business, Maguire Health Insurance Services, was consistently one of the most successful insurance agencies in San Diego County.

She now lives in Ramona, California, where Arlene enjoys the good life, keeping busy with many friends, a remarkably close-knit family, and her loveable cat, Misty (star of her own YouTube channel @ShariLikesFruit).

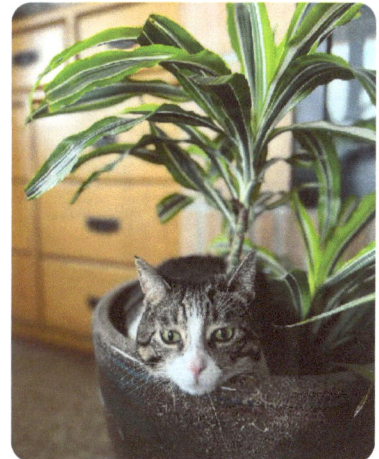

www.ingramcontent.com/pod-product-compliance
Lightning Source LLC
Chambersburg PA
CBHW061048090426
42740CB00002B/80